Arranged by GAIL LEW and CHRIS LOBDELL

CONTENTS

TITLE	PAGE

Editor: **Gail Lew**
Production Coordinator: **Karl Bork**
MIDI and CD Background Orchestrations: **Chris Lobdell**
Art Design: **Ernesto Ebanks**
Book Art Layout: **Michael Ramsay**

From the Motion Pictures "STAR WARS" and "THE EMPIRE STRIKES BACK"
A Lucasfilm Ltd. Production-A Twentieth Century Fox Release

Star Wars
(Main Title)

Music by **JOHN WILLIAMS**
Arranged by GAIL LEW
and CHRIS LOBDELL

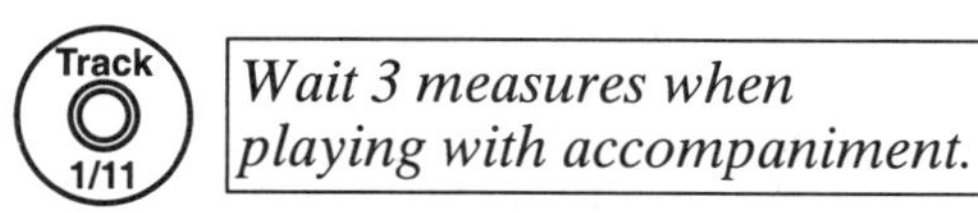

Majestic march tempo

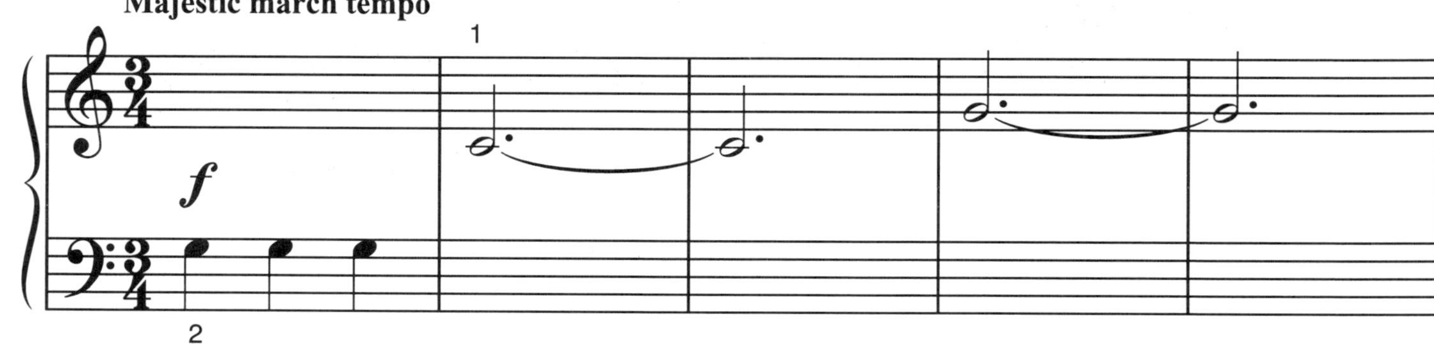

Accompaniment *(student plays one octave higher)*

11
l.h. cross over
2

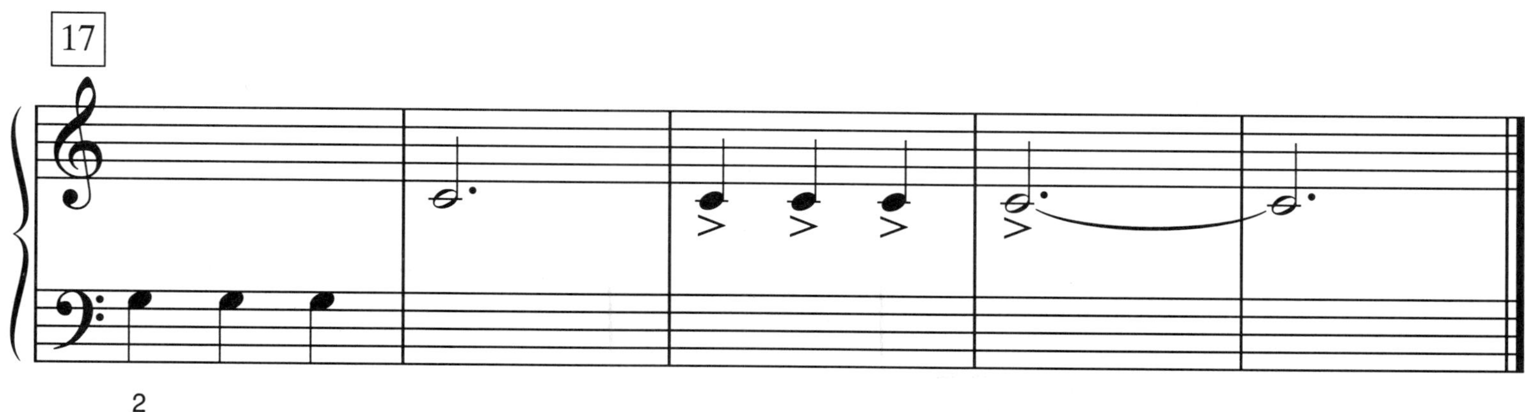
17
2

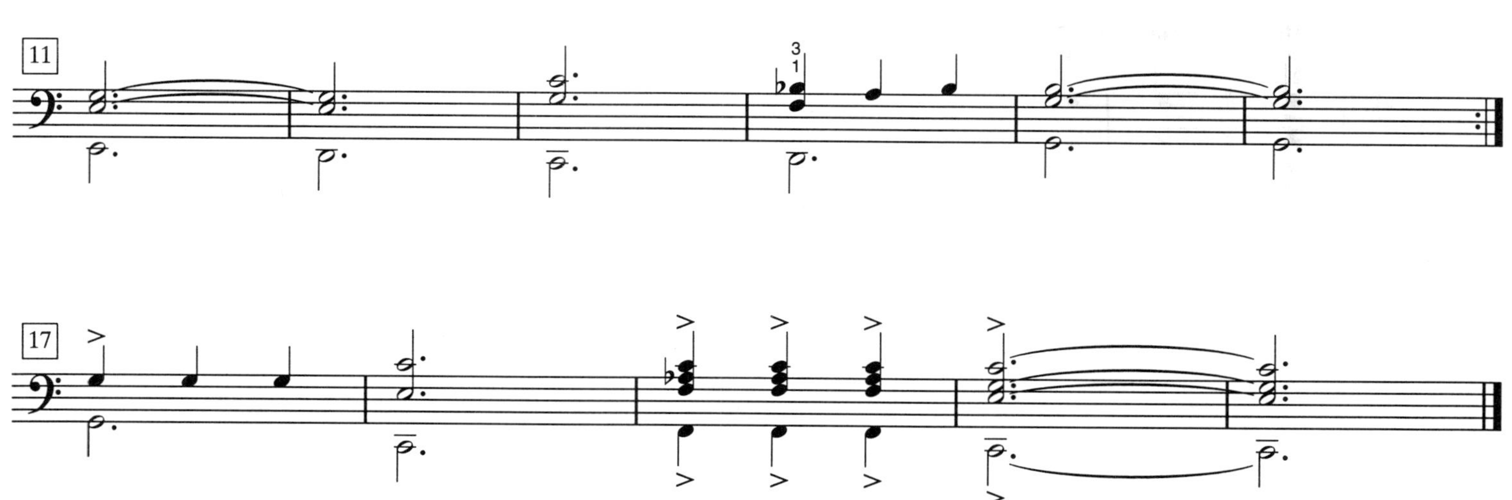
11
17
3
1

Theme from "Superman"

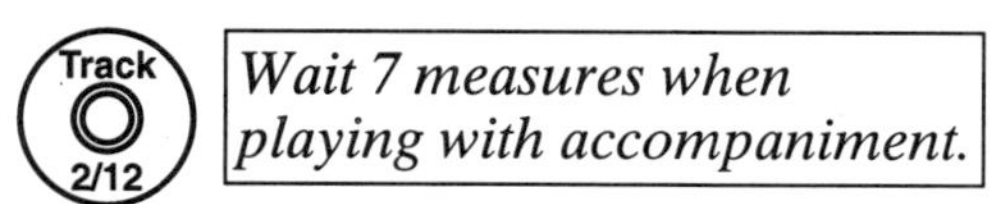

Accompaniment (*student plays one octave higher*)

5
ELM05005

Over the Rainbow

Words by E.Y. HARBURG

Music by HAROLD ARLEN
*Arranged by GAIL LEW
and CHRIS LOBDELL*

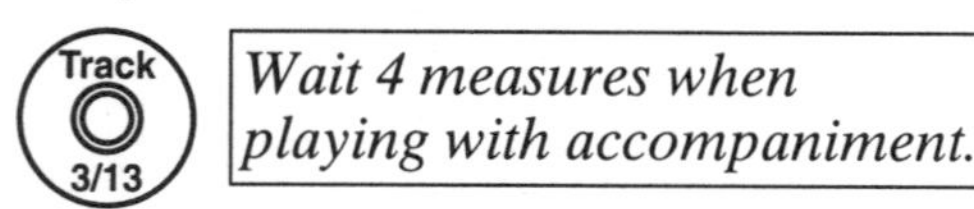

*Wait 4 measures when
playing with accompaniment.*

Andante

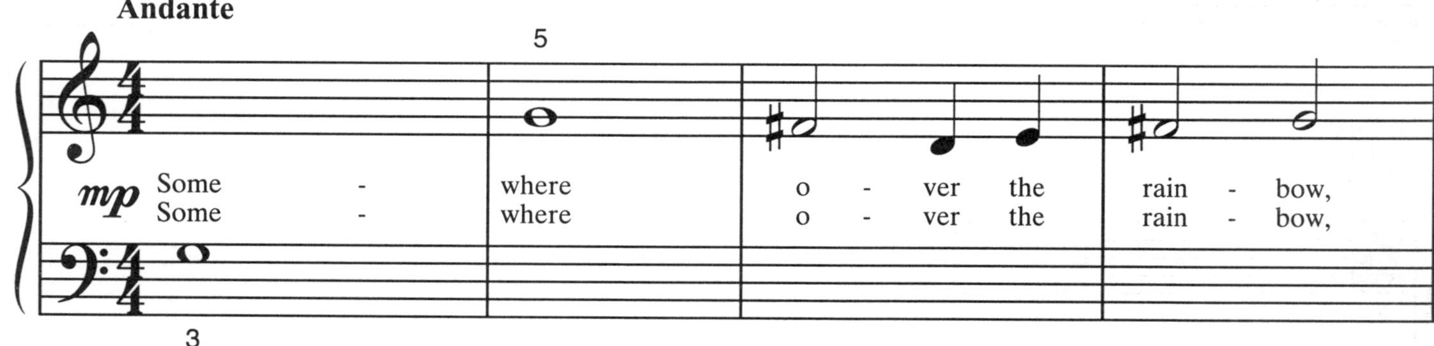

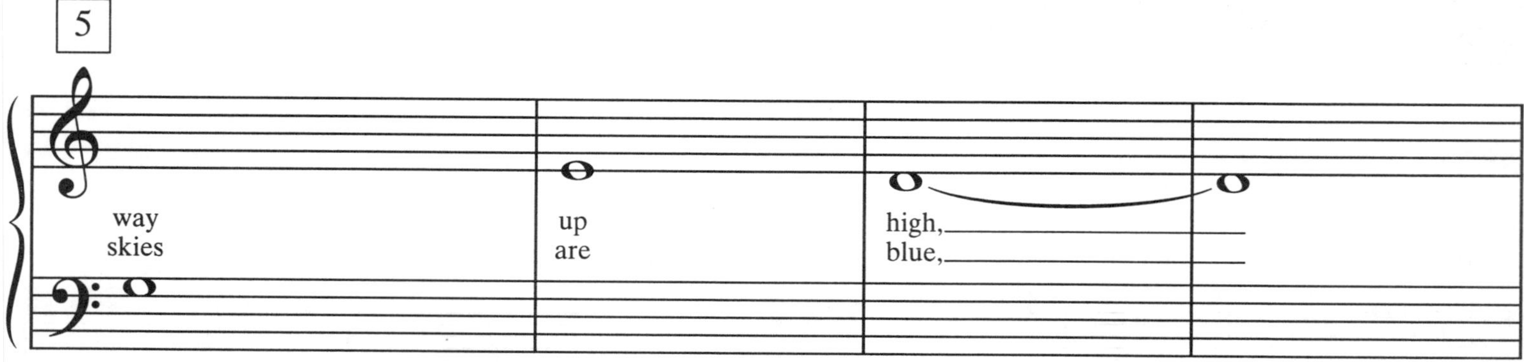

Accompaniment *(student plays one octave higher)*

9
there's
and
a
the
land
dreams
that
that
I
you
heard
dare
of
to

13
once
dream
in
real - ly
a
lul - la -
do
come
by.
true.
4

R1

R5
1
2

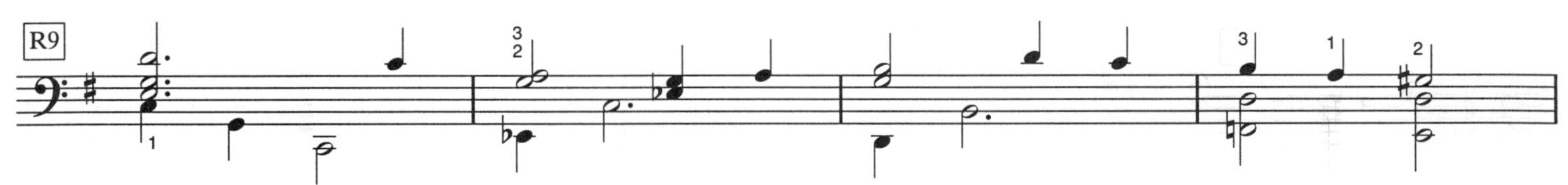
R9
3
2
1
3
1
2

R13
1

The Lion Sleeps Tonight

New Lyrics and Revised Music by
GEORGE DAVID WEISS, HUGO PERETTI
and **LUIGI CREATORE**
*Arranged by GAIL LEW
and CHRIS LOBDELL*

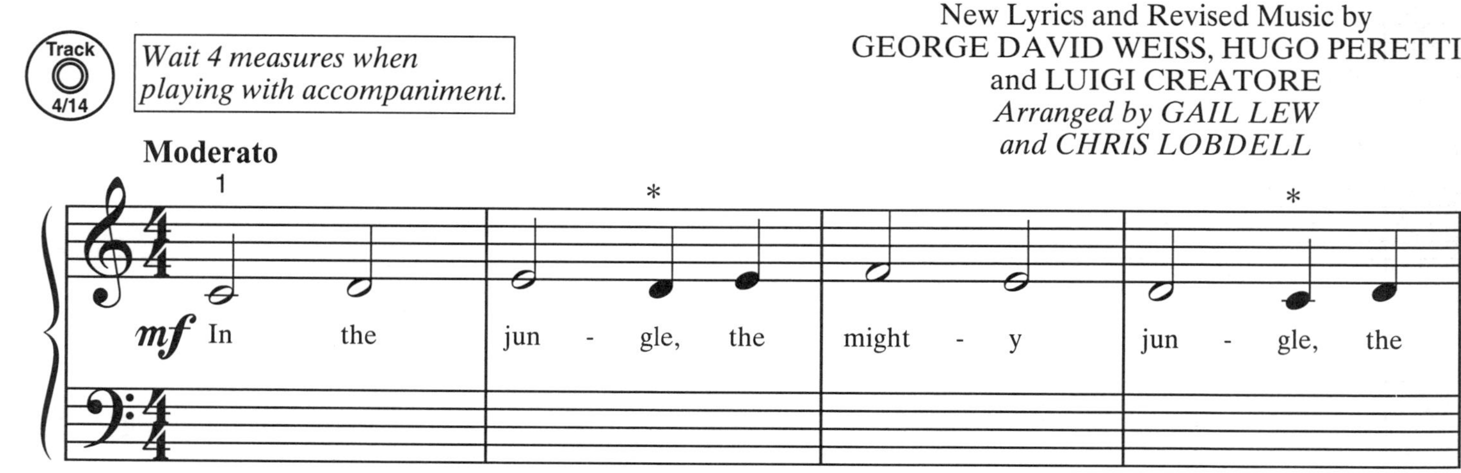

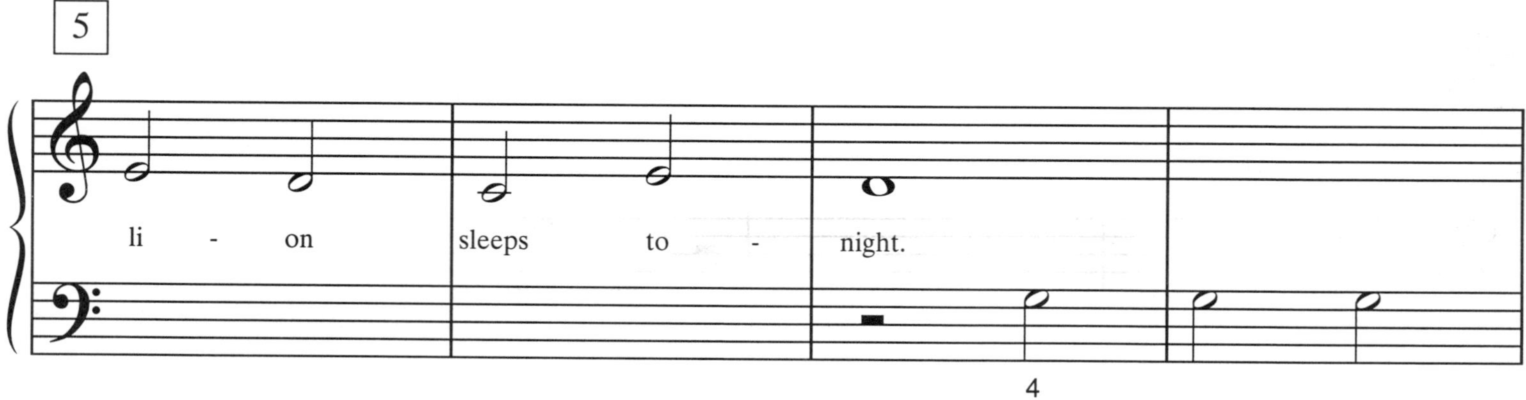

*Dotted rhythm (♩ ♪) may be taught by rote at the discretion of the teacher.

Accompaniment (*student plays one octave higher*)

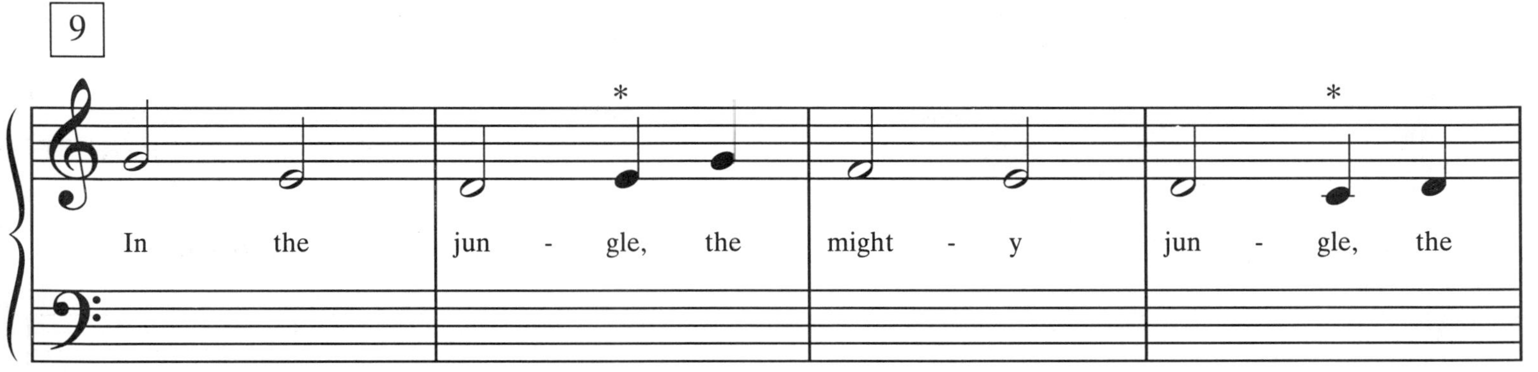
9
In the jun - gle, the might - y jun - gle, the

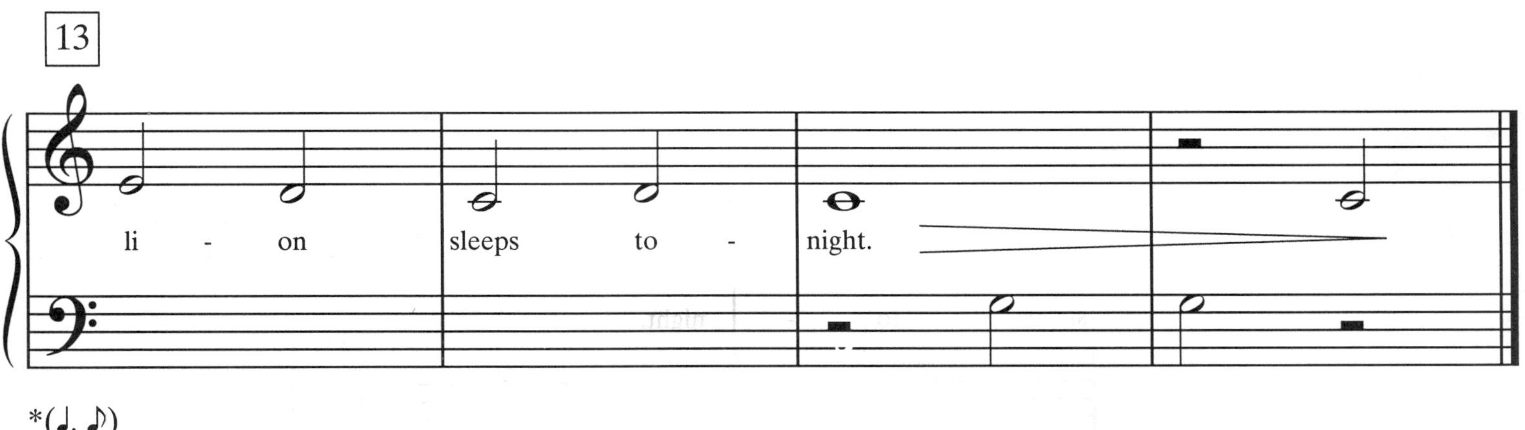
13
li - on sleeps to - night.
*(♩. ♪)

9

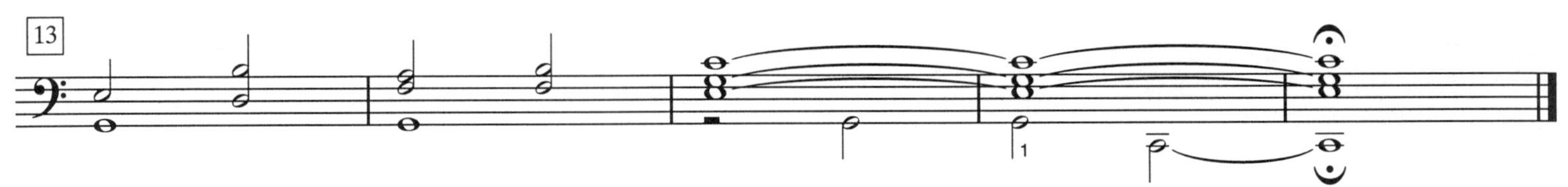
13

James Bond Theme

Wait 8 measures when playing with accompaniment.

Track 5/15

Music by MONTY NORMAN
Arranged by GAIL LEW
and CHRIS LOBDELL

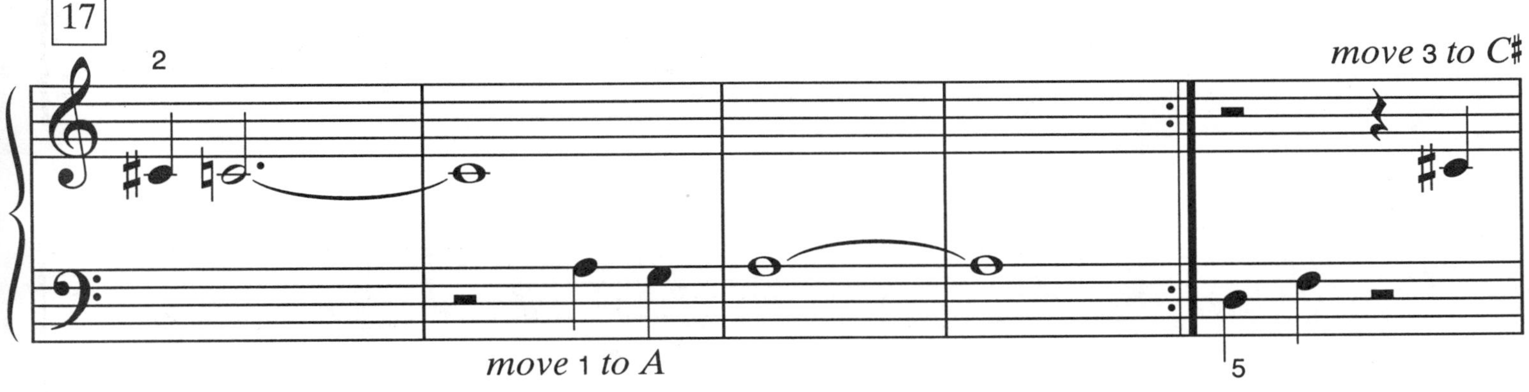

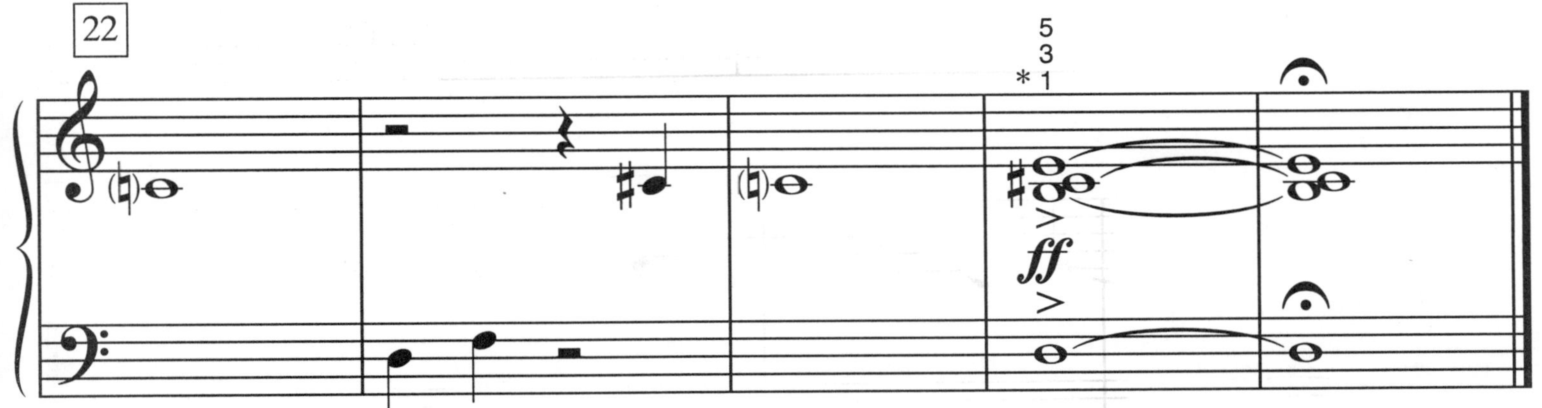

*Right-hand chord (B-C#-E) is optional and may be introduced at the discretion of the teacher.

Scooby-Doo, Where Are You?

Words and Music by
DAVID MOOK and BEN RALEIGH
*Arranged by GAIL LEW
and CHRIS LOBDELL*

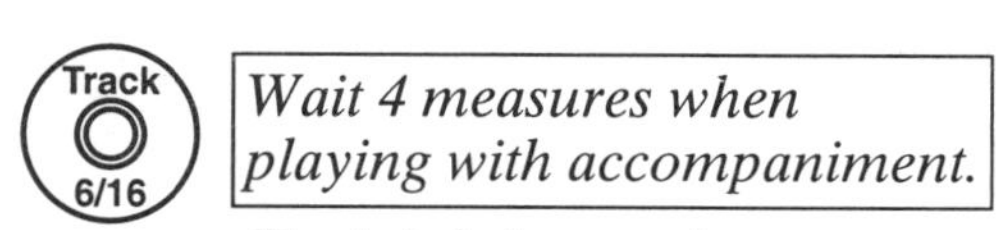

Fast driving rock

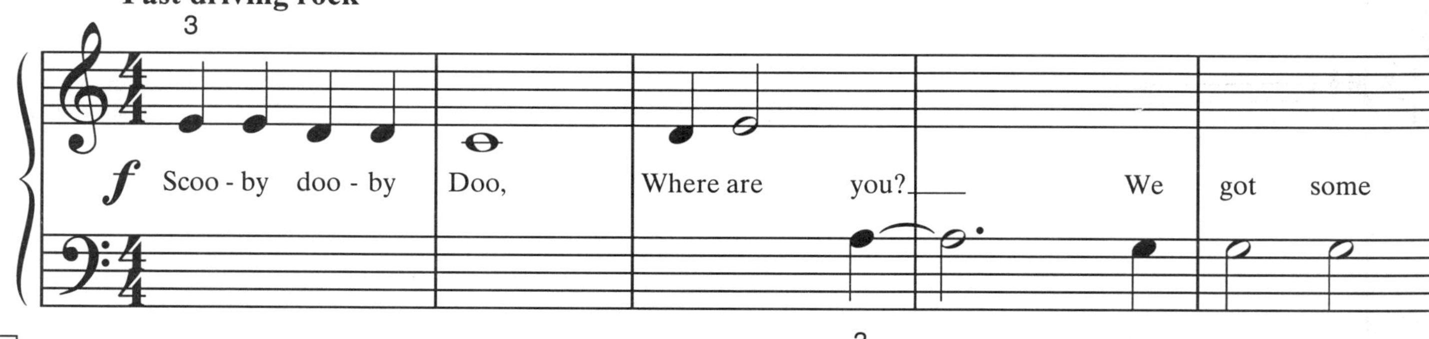

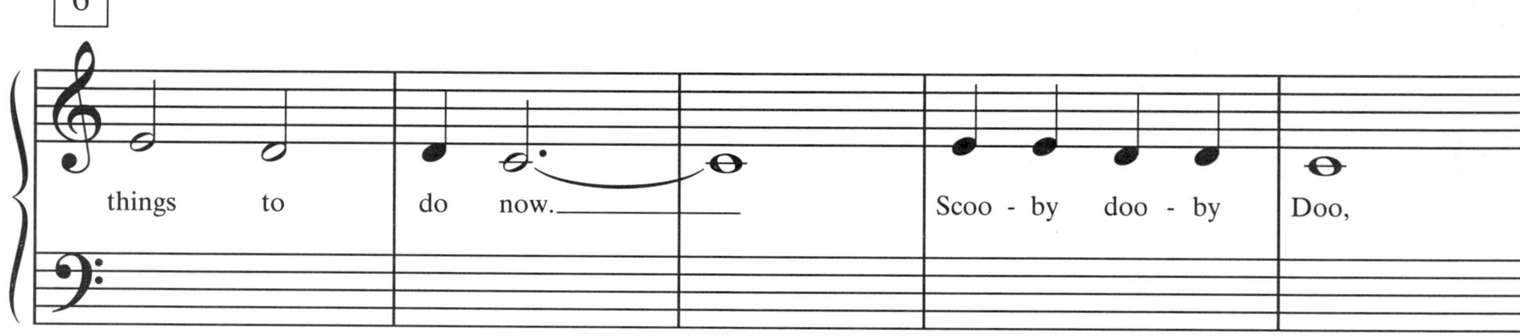

Accompaniment *(student plays one octave higher)*

ELM05005

17
Come on, Scoo - by Doo, I see you pre - tend - ing you've
Scoo - by doo - by Doo, here are you. You're read - y

22
got a sliv - er. But you're not fool - ing me, 'cause I can see
and you're will - ing. If we can count on you, Scoo - by - Doo,

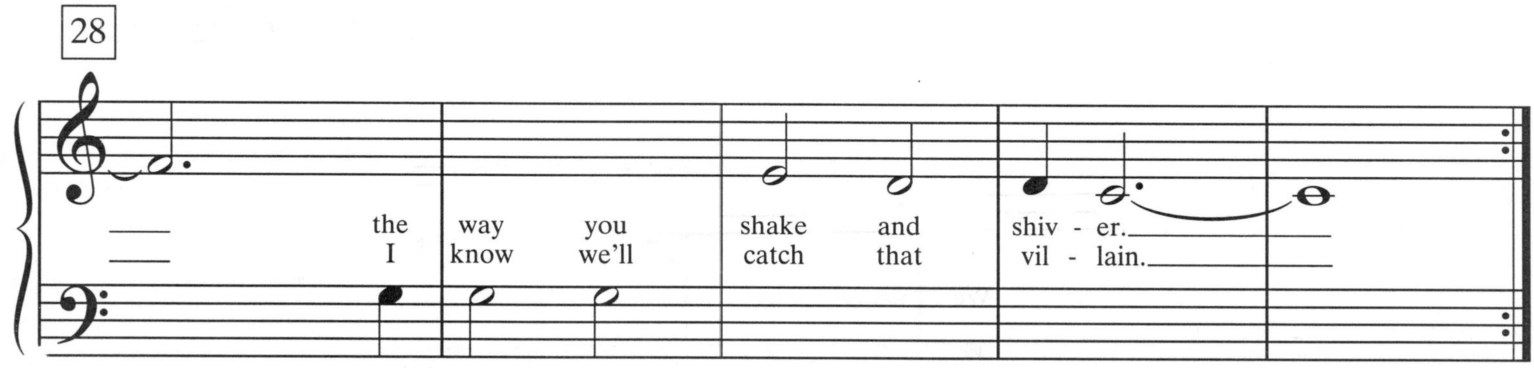
28
the way you shake and shiv - er.
I know we'll catch that vil - lain.

17
22
28

Theme Song from the Mirisch-G&E Production, "THE PINK PANTHER," a United Artist's Release

The Pink Panther

Music by
HENRY MANCINI
*Arranged by GAIL LEW
and CHRIS LOBDELL*

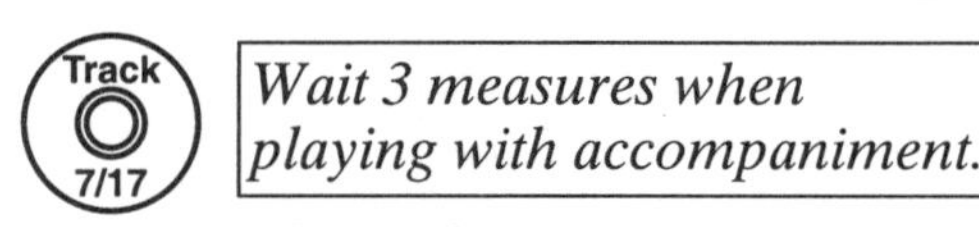

*Wait 3 measures when
playing with accompaniment.*

Mysterioso

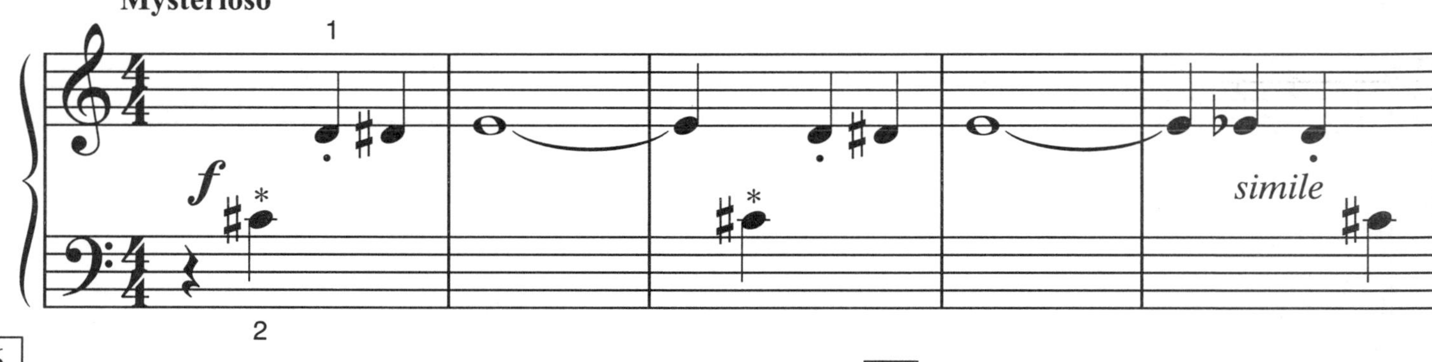

*Dotted rhythm (♪ ♩.) may be taught by rote at the discretion of the teacher.

**Long-short rhythm (♩. ♪) may be taught by rote.

Accompaniment *(student plays one octave higher)*

*(♪ ♩.)

**Long-short rhythm (♩. ♪) may be taught by rote.

ELM05005

Fawkes the Phoenix

Music by
JOHN WILLIAMS
*Arranged by GAIL LEW
and CHRIS LOBDELL*

Wait 4 measures when playing with accompaniment.

Moderato

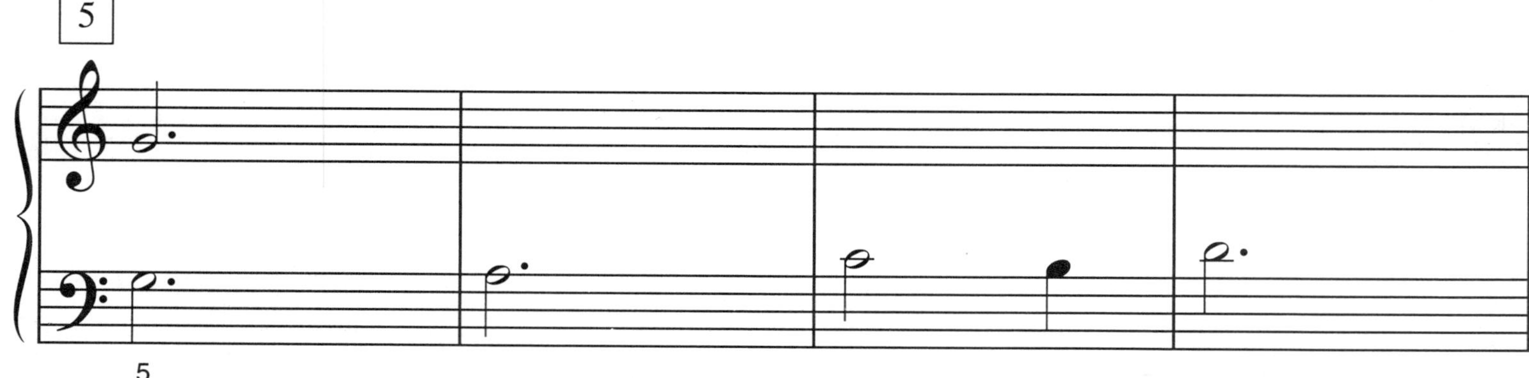

Accompaniment *(student plays one octave higher)*

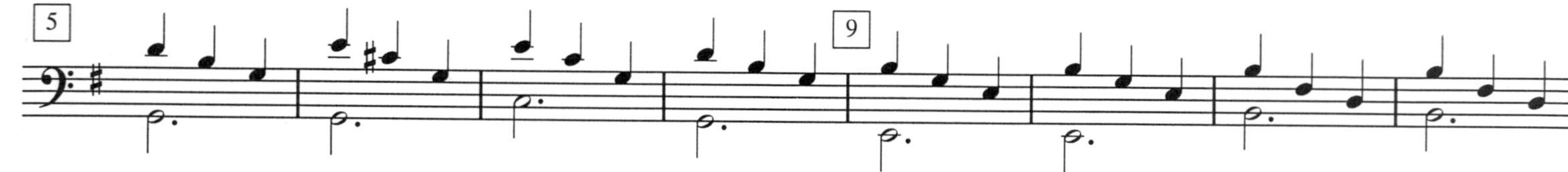

18
25
30
35
40
25
30
35
40
ELM05005

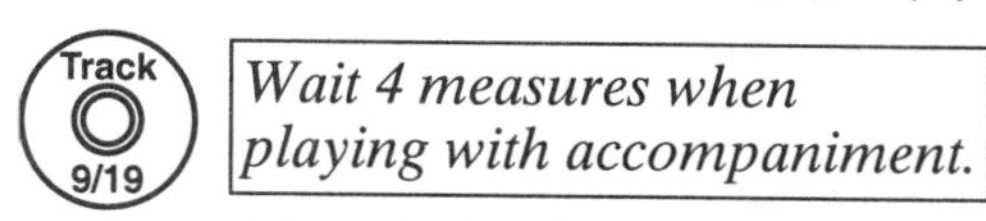

From "HARRY POTTER AND THE PRISONER OF AZKABAN"

A Window to the Past

Music by
JOHN WILLIAMS
*Arranged by GAIL LEW
and CHRIS LOBDELL*

*Wait 4 measures when
playing with accompaniment.*

Nostalgically

*Dotted rhythm (♩. ♪) may be taught by rote at the discretion of the teacher.

Accompaniment *(student plays one octave higher)*

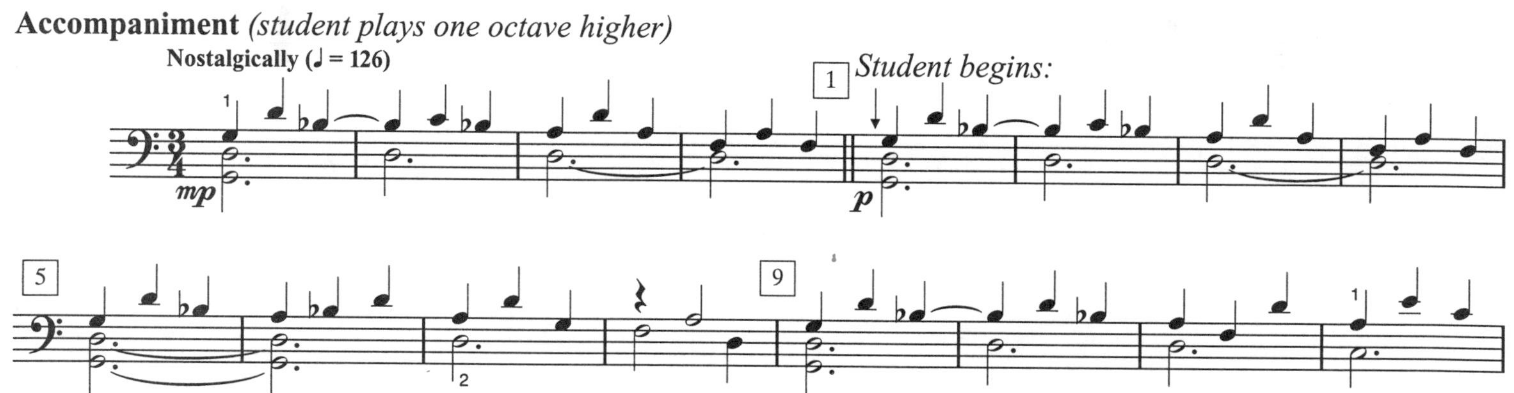

ELM05005

13
17
move 5 to D
21
Nobly
move 1 to B
mp
*(♩. ♪)
13
17
21
Nobly

26
31
3
*
*
35
*(♩. ♪)
26
31
2
35
rit.
ELM05005
21

Hedwig's Theme

Music by
JOHN WILLIAMS
Arranged by GAIL LEW
and CHRIS LOBDELL

Wait 4 measures when playing with accompaniment.

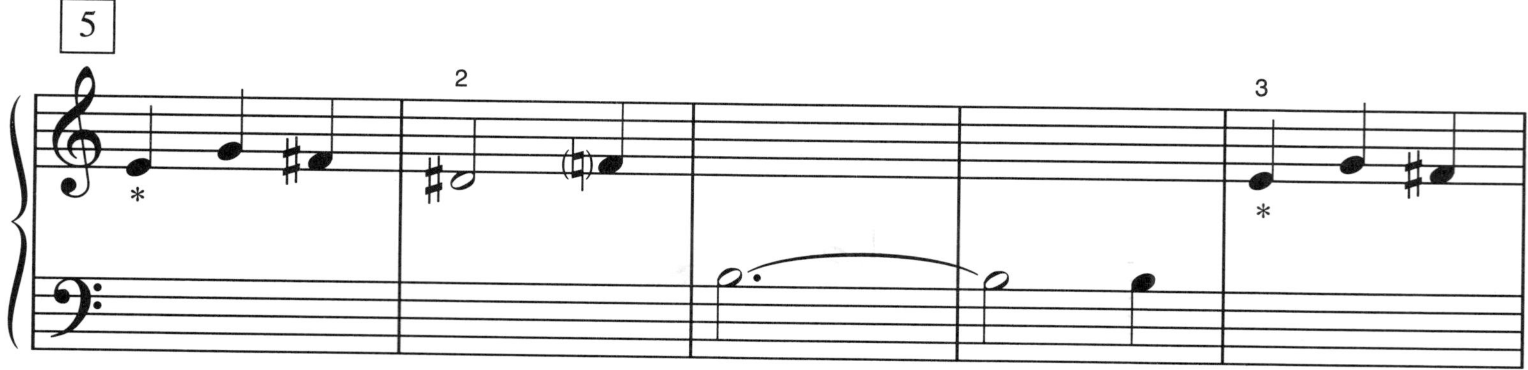

*Dotted rhythm (♩. ♪) may be taught by rote at the discretion of the teacher.

Accompaniment *(student plays one octave higher)*

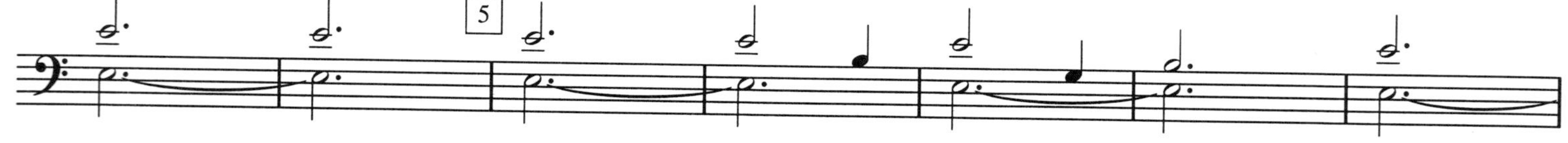

10
move 3 to A♭
3
2
1
3

15
4
*(♩. ♪)

10
15
2

24
20
2
*
3
5
25
3
*
2
1
move 3 to G
3
*(♩. ♪)
20
25
30
ELM05005